Canada's Trees

Elizabeth MacLeod

Scholastic Canada Ltd.

Toronto New York London Auckland Sydney
Mexico City New Delhi Hong Kong Buenos Aires

With much love for Jane, a true tree lover. Special thanks to my "tree-rific" editor Tamara Sztainbok. Love always to Paul, who can charm the birds out of the trees!
— Elizabeth MacLeod

Many thanks to Kristjan Vitols (Supervisor, Tree Nursery & Natural Resources Management, Urban Forestry, Parks, Forestry & Recreation, City of Toronto) for reviewing this book.

Scholastic Canada Ltd.
604 King Street West, Toronto, Ontario M5V 1E1, Canada

Scholastic Inc.
557 Broadway, New York, NY 10012, USA

Scholastic Australia Pty Limited
PO Box 579, Gosford, NSW 2250, Australia

Scholastic New Zealand Limited
Private Bag 94407, Botany, Manukau 2163, New Zealand

Scholastic Children's Books
Euston House, 24 Eversholt Street, London NW1 1DB, UK

Library and Archives Canada Cataloguing in Publication

MacLeod, Elizabeth
Canada's trees / Elizabeth MacLeod.

(Canada close up)
Includes index.
ISBN 978-1-4431-0739-6

1. Trees--Canada--Juvenile literature. 2. Trees--Ecology--Canada--Juvenile literature. I. Title. II. Series: Canada close up (Toronto, Ont.)

QK201.M33 2011   j582.160971   C2011-901361-4

6 5 4 3 2 1   Printed in Canada 119   11 12 13 14 15 16

EcoLogo

Certified Lithographic Printing
Services CCD-041

Table of Contents

Pronunciation Guide

a as in cat; **ah** as in call; **ee** as in see; **eh** as in pet; **i** as in pit; **oh** as in ocean; **oo** as in food; **ur** as in fur; **uh** as in but

Terrific Trees

Canada is famous for its **forests** and trees. People couldn't live without these beautiful, big plants. They produce oxygen, which we breathe, they absorb noise to quiet our neighbourhoods and they filter pollution out of rain water. They also provide us with firewood, food and medicine.

That's not all. Wood for buildings and furniture, as well as pulp for paper, come from trees. Their shade cools the air in summer. During winter, they protect people and animals from cold and wind. Tree roots help prevent soil from washing away.

The trees in this book are **native** trees — that means they grow here naturally. Turn the page to learn more about Canada's terrific trees.

Chapter 1

Maples

In the fall a forest of maple trees is a beautiful place to be. The leaves glow with dazzling reds, brilliant oranges and bright yellows.

It's easy to tell maples from other trees. Can you picture the leaf on Canada's flag? That's how most maple leaves look. They're divided into segments called **lobes**. The leaf on Canada's flag has five lobes: two small ones at the bottom, one large one in the middle and one on each side. The points on the lobes are called **teeth**.

Maple trees are called broadleaf trees. They have wide leaves, not thin, needle-like ones. Birches, oaks, poplars and willows are broadleaf trees, too. They're also called **deciduous** (di-SIJ-oo-uhss) trees. Almost all deciduous trees lose their leaves when winter is coming.

Deciduous trees lose their leaves in winter.

Maple leaves grow best in lots of light. If you take a close look at the leaf stalks, also called **petioles** (PEHT-ee-ohls), you'll see some of them are twisted. They curl around so the leaves face up and can get lots of light.

BIG, BIG LEAVES

Leaves on most bigleaf maples are 15 to 30 centimetres wide. That's as big as a medium pizza. And some bigleaf maple leaves are twice that size!

You'll find maple trees all across the country. There are 10 **species** (SPEE-sees) or types that grow naturally in Canada. Some maples grow to be 45 metres tall, or about as tall as a 15-storey building!

Did you know the leaf on Canada's flag is a sugar maple leaf? These maples are Canada's biggest source of maple syrup and maple sugar. Maple syrup and sugar are made from **sap** — liquid that carries water and food through a tree. Hundreds of years ago, Canada's Native peoples learned how to boil sap to make sweet syrup.

MMMMM MAPLE SYRUP

It takes about 40 litres of maple sap to make 1 litre of syrup!

The Manitoba maple is the only maple that doesn't have a typical maple leaf. This tree's leaf looks as if it's made up of lots of little leaves or leaflets.

Leaves on a Manitoba maple

Have you ever watched maple keys twirl down to the ground like tiny helicopters? Maple trees are some of the few trees that have seeds like this. The wind can carry the seeds far from their tree. Maple keys, also called **samara** (SAM-uh-ruh), are the tree's **fruit**.

Maple keys

Maple trees have strong wood, so it's used for houses, furniture — and baseball bats! Crafters like to carve bowls, platters and more from this beautiful wood. Musical instruments such as guitars and pianos are made from maple wood because it carries sound waves well.

Birds and other animals also use maple trees. They eat maple keys, buds and twigs.

Chapter 2

Pines

Walk through a forest of pine trees. Even in winter, you're surrounded by a fresh, sharp smell and green branches. That's because pine trees are **evergreen** — they stay green all year.

Pine trees are also called **coniferous** (kon-IF-ur-uhs). That means they have **cones** full of seeds and their leaves are usually needle-shaped and green all year. Cones can be anywhere from 2 to 60 centimetres long, or about from the size of one of your knuckles to longer than your arm!

This lodgepole pine has both female (left) and male (right) cones.

Many conifers have needle-like leaves. But pine trees are the only ones that have their needles in bundles of two, three or five. And pine needles are much longer than most other tree needles.

MORE CONIFERS

Like pines, spruce trees, firs and cedars are conifers (KON-uh-furs). They all have cones, needles for leaves and needles that stay green all year round. Larches are also conifers, although their needles change colour and drop in the fall.

There are nine species of pines native to Canada. The lodgepole pine is Alberta's provincial tree. Native peoples used this tree for poles to support their lodges or teepees, giving it its name. Its twisted needles grow in pairs.

The eastern white pine is the provincial tree of Ontario. It's also the tallest tree in eastern Canada. This pine's needles are in bundles of five. It's easy to remember that when you're in a forest trying to identify a pine: there are as many needles in this tree's bundles as there are letters in the word "white."

Pines can live for many years. Whitebark pines live for 500 years and ponderosa pines live almost that long. "Ponderosa" is Spanish for large — the needles on this tree can be longer than your hand!

Ponderosa pine needles

Pines are attacked by many pests. The mountain pine beetle has killed millions of pine trees from British Columbia to Saskatchewan and will likely kill millions more. Bark beetles attack pine bark, and the white pine weevil deforms white pines. Rust diseases can damage the branches, and some butterflies and moths eat pine needles.

Hundreds of years ago, some pines were important for use as ship masts. And for a long time, Native peoples have made and decorated baskets and trays with pine needles.

Today pines are used for lumber, furniture, making paper — and for Christmas trees. Pine trees are also known for a liquid called **resin** that they produce. Resin is used to make turpentine, which is important for thinning paint and other uses.

Chapter 3

Oaks

If you spot a tree with leaves that look like they have fingers, you're probably looking at an oak. The leaves of some oaks have fingers, or lobes, that are pointed. Others have round-tipped lobes.

Even in the winter you can check out oak leaves. Although these trees are deciduous, the dead leaves often stay on the branches over winter.

CANADA'S OAKS

black oak
bur oak
chinquapin oak
dwarf chinquapin oak
Garry oak
northern pin oak
pin oak
red oak
Shumard oak
swamp white oak

A sure way to tell if a tree is an oak is to look along its branches for acorns. These are smooth, thick-walled nuts with a cuplike base or cap. They can be about as small as one of your fingernails or as long as your baby finger.

Bur oak acorns

Some acorns are plump and round, while others are long and thin. Most acorn caps are tough and scaly but the bur oak has a hairy cap.

The acorn is an oak tree's fruit. The fruit you see on many Canadian trees doesn't look like the fruit you're used to eating. But like most fruit, the seeds are inside. For instance, there is one seed inside each acorn.

Many wild animals love to eat acorns. Acorns are full of proteins and minerals. Birds, including woodpeckers and some ducks, feast on them and so do other animals, such as mice, squirrels and even bears and deer!

Acorns that have been left behind by animals can sprout into trees.

With its reddish buds, twigs and wood, it's obvious how the red oak gets its name. This oak grows in provinces east of Manitoba and it's Prince Edward Island's provincial tree.

FOREST FIRE!

It's hard to believe, but some trees depend on forest fires to grow. Garry oaks are short trees that can survive fires, but don't grow well in shade. Fires burn and remove trees that would overshadow these oaks.

Don't ever start a forest fire. There are enough fires that begin naturally — from lightning striking trees, for instance.

Sometimes growths that look like small apples, and are called "oak apples," form on oak branches around wasp eggs laid there. These "apples" can be as large as small plums and can be brown, green or red. They provide food for wasp eggs when they hatch.

The wood of oak trees is pink to reddish brown and well-known for its strength and beauty. It's used to make top-quality furniture and flooring. Some oaks have waterproof wood, which is good for making barrels.

Chapter 4

SPRUCES

Like most conifers, a spruce tree has one straight trunk, growing tall up to the sky. Native spruces also have short needles, small, plump cones and thin, scaly bark. Their branches usually grow straight and horizontal.

Most spruces have shallow roots. Because of this, they can grow in northern Canada where there's only a thin layer of soil that doesn't stay frozen all year. As well, spruces don't need full sun to grow well.

Sitka spruces are the tallest conifers in Canada. Many grow 55 metres high and can live for 800 years. You find them in British Columbia and they're named for the area of Alaska where they also grow.

Did you know that the tallest tree in the country is a Sitka spruce? It's called the Carmanah (carr-MANN-ah) Giant and it soars 95 metres tall. That's taller than a 30-storey building and it may be the tallest spruce in the world!

Sitka spruce

Because Sitka spruces are so tall, their branches are spaced far apart up the tree. Fewer branches mean fewer knot holes in the timber, which makes for better, stronger wood. That's why, during the Second World War, airplanes were made from Sitka spruce wood.

With their thin, scaly bark, spruce trees are easily damaged in fires. Because of their shallow roots, spruces can be knocked over or broken by strong winds.

Three spruces are provincial trees. The white spruce represents Manitoba, while the black spruce is Newfoundland and Labrador's provincial tree. Nova Scotia's provincial tree is the red spruce.

The cones of the black spruce become purplish brown. They open in a flash and their seeds pop out when the heat of a forest fire warms them.

Animals appreciate spruce trees —
porcupines nibble on their bark and
birds and mice snack on their buds
and seeds. Many animals huddle under
their branches. Others shelter high in
the **crown**, or top of the tree, where the
branches may grow close together.

ANIMALS NEED TREES

Trees provide food, shelter and homes for insects,
birds and other animals. Almost every part of a
tree can be food for animals: bark, buds, cones,
fruit, leaves, nuts, seeds and shoots.

Spruce wood is used in construction,
building homes and to make boxes and
musical instruments. No other native
Canadian trees produce as much lumber.
It's also broken down into fibres to make
pulp for paper. As well, spruce wood is
used for crates and baskets that hold food
because it has almost no taste or smell.

Chapter 5

Birches

When you think of birch trees, you probably think of their bark. Not every birch has papery bark but they all have horizontal markings on their trunks.

CANADA'S BIRCHES

Alaska paper birch
blueleaf birch
cherry birch
gray birch
Kenai birch
mountain paper birch
water birch
white birch
yellow birch

These deciduous trees have leaves shaped like ragged teardrops. The pointed tip helps drain off rain.

Native peoples have made canoes from birch bark for thousands of years. That's because sticky oils in the bark make it strong but flexible. Birch bark is also lightweight and waterproof.

Like your skin, bark protects everything that's inside. It keeps out insects and diseases. It also protects the tree from fires and sudden temperature changes.

Don't ever damage a tree's bark. It doesn't heal the way your skin does. When you hurt bark, it's easy for infection to get in and kill the tree.

Birch leaves are shaped like teardrops.

BIRCH SYRUP?

Did you know some people make syrup for pancakes and waffles from birch trees? It tastes rich and spicy, and uses more than twice as much sap as it takes to make maple syrup!

There are nine species of birches in Canada. The white birch has creamy, paper-like bark. This is the main tree used for canoes. This birch is found in every province and territory and is Saskatchewan's provincial tree.

Not all birches have white bark. The yellow birch has yellowish bark and is Quebec's provincial tree. The bark of the cherry birch is dark cherry coloured.

Bark of a yellow birch

Two insects that damage birch trees are the bronze birch borer and the birch leaf miner.

Birches can also be hit by a condition called birch dieback. It turns leaves yellow and kills branches from the top of the tree down until the tree dies. All birch trees need lots of water and nutrients to stay healthy.

Birch wood is beautiful and pale, so it's often used for making furniture.

SUN LOVERS

Most birches don't like shade. So after a forest is cleared by logging or fire, birch trees are usually the first ones to grow there again.

Chapter 6

Firs

Straight trunk with a pointed tip, plump cones and short, flat needles — that's a fir tree. It's easy to tell a fir from other conifers because most are shaped like tall, slim triangles.

Four firs are native to Canada. They all grow well in shade and can survive in soil that has few minerals or nutrients. However firs become very weak if they dry out during a drought. They also have to fight such pests as the eastern spruce budworm, which eats buds, and the hemlock looper, which eats fir needles.

New Brunswick's provincial tree is the balsam fir. It's the only fir tree native to eastern Canada. Some trees need lots of space around them but not these. Balsam firs can grow so close together that it's tough to walk between them.

Balsam firs often grow among other trees, such as white spruces and white birches, as you see here.

This fir is a popular choice for Christmas trees because its fresh-smelling needles stay on the tree so long. In a forest, the needles may stay on for as long as twenty years! Fir trees are also used to make paper and lumber.

A FIR THAT ISN'T A FIR

The Douglas-fir looks a lot like a fir, but it's not. It belongs in a group of its own. It can grow to more than 115 metres high — that's taller than a 37-storey building — and live for over 1000 years. You'll find it in British Columbia and Alberta.

Fir tree cones stand up on the twig and have scales with two seeds each. Some tree seeds sprout as soon as they fall to the ground. Others, such as fir (and spruce) seeds, sprout only if they're moist and cool for a time, through winter's cold and snow.

Many animals depend on firs. Squirrels love their seeds and many birds and other animals hide or shelter from the snow under their low branches.

Chapter 7

Aspens, Cottonwoods and Poplars

Thanks to their similar leaves, flowers, fruit and seeds, scientists group aspen, cottonwood and poplar trees together. The fruit and flowers on these trees hang down in long bunches called **catkins**.

CANADA'S ASPENS, COTTONWOODS AND POPLARS

Largetooth Aspen
Trembling Aspen
Black Cottonwood
Eastern Cottonwood
Narrowleaf Cottonwood
Balsam Poplar

This group of trees likes to grow in open, sunny spots. That makes them some of the first trees to begin growing in open areas left by fires or tree clearings. Their wood is used for furniture, boxes and matchsticks, as well as for pulp for making paper.

The seeds of these trees have a tuft of white fluff like cotton attached to them. Cottonwood trees get their name from this silky tuft. It helps the seeds float through air so they can begin growing in new places far from their original tree.

Fluffy cottonwood seeds

Most aspen, cottonwood and poplar leaves are wide and shaped a bit like triangles. However the narrowleaf cottonwood gets its name from its long, thin leaves. You'll only find this tree in Saskatchewan and Alberta.

In the slightest breeze, the leaves of the trembling aspen flutter and tremble. These leaves shake more than others because the stalk, or petiole, that attaches it to the twig is flat, so it cuts easily through the air. This tree is found almost everywhere in Canada except the far north.

Aspen, cottonwood and poplar leaves turn golden in fall. As summer ends, days shorten, which tells trees winter is coming. In spring and summer, a substance in the leaves called **chlorophyll** (KLOHR-uh-fill) helps trees make food. Chlorophyll makes leaves green.

Golden leaves on aspen trees

But in the fall, leaves stop making food and
the chlorophyll disappears. You start to
see the yellows and oranges hidden there.
Red leaves are caused by the presence of a
sugar called glucose (GLOO-cohs).

Chapter 8

Larches

No coniferous trees lose their needles in fall — none, that is, except larches. These trees have cones like other conifers, but their needles turn bright yellow in fall and drop.

CANADA'S LARCHES

subalpine larch
tamarack larch
western larch

How else are larches different? In other conifers, the needles grow in groups of up to five. Larch needles grow 15 to 60 in a bunch, so they look like bristly tufts.

Subalpine larches

Three larches are native to Canada and they all grow best in lots of sun. Their cones are no longer than one of your fingers.

The tamarack larch lives in every province and territory. Tamarack is an Algonquin First Nations people's word — hackmatack is another Algonquin name for this larch. Hack is also a name for this tree, perhaps because the tree is easy to chop, or hack. This tree is the official tree of the Northwest Territories.

Tamarack larches grow even in the tundra.

For thousands of years, Native peoples have used larch roots to sew their canoes. Roots are an important part of every tree. They help it take in and store water, nutrients and air from the soil, which trees need to survive. Roots also anchor trees so they can survive strong winds.

Some roots grow just below the soil surface, while others stretch down as deep as the tree is tall. Roots normally grow out three times as far as the branches spread out. As they grow old and thick, they may even crack brick walls and lift sidewalks!

LARGEST LARCH

The world's biggest larch is the western larch. It grows in southeastern British Columbia and into Alberta. Soaring as much as 70 metres high — that's about as tall as a 23-storey building — this tree can live 400 years.

The wood of the larch tree is strong and rot-resistant, so it's used for bridges and to build boats. Some people carve duck decoys out of small larch branches.

Larches can lose their needles to the larch sawfly pest. Others are damaged by porcupines snacking on the bark.

Chapter 9

Willows

They're some of the first trees to leaf out in spring and the last to shed their leaves in fall. Willows are deciduous trees with spreading crowns and long, slim, pointed leaves.

CANADA'S WILLOWS

Bebb willow
black willow
Pacific willow
peachleaf willow
pussy willow
shining willow

You know spring is coming when you see fluffy grey pussy willows. The trees they grow on, also called pussy willows, grow in every province. They're Canada's best-known native willows. Scientists call the furry pussy willows catkins.

Pussy willows

Did you know those little grey pussy willows are clusters of flowers? Not all flowers on trees have bright petals. Some flowers are tiny or buried in the leaves. Tree flowers are often pale, not colourful like many other flowers.

Usually the flowers appear on trees in the spring, around the same time as the leaves. The flowers quickly fade but seeds and fruit grow from the flowers. Willow seeds ride winds and water thanks to the fluff on them.

Often on willow tips you'll see growths that look like pine cones. These growths, called galls, are made by a tiny fly called a willow pinecone gall midge. The galls look odd but they don't kill the tree.

The Bebb willow is Canada's most widespread native willow — it's found right across the country. You can identify this willow by the diamond-shaped patches you'll often see on its trunk. For thousands of years, Native peoples have woven baskets from this willow's twigs and branches.

A Bebb willow

PEACHY LEAVES

Most willow leaves are long and thin. But the leaves of the peachleaf willow are wider with a long tip and look a lot like peach tree leaves. The peachleaf willow is the tallest native willow in the Prairies and grows from British Columbia to Quebec.

Willow wood is used to make paper, crates and boxes. Long ago, Native peoples learned that the bark has a pain-killing drug in it. Moose depend on willow twigs for winter food.

Chapter 10

Cedars

Canada's history might have been very different without the cedar tree. Back in 1535, French explorer Jacques Cartier and his crew were dying from scurvy, a disease caused by not eating enough vitamin C.

Native people taught the Frenchmen to make "tea" from cedar bark and leaves.

This liquid contained vitamin C and saved the lives of Cartier and his men. Cartier went on to explore the St. Lawrence River.

Cedar leaves look like small scales. They grow in flat sprays that are shaped like fans. Cedar cones are small, only about the size of your thumbnail. These coniferous trees grow slowly but can live for hundreds of years. They like moist soil and sometimes live in swamps.

Two cedars are native to Canada. The western redcedar is British Columbia's provincial tree. Its bark is reddish and it lives in British Columbia and Alberta. These are tall trees — some are up to 60 metres tall. Native peoples have built huge dugout canoes from them.

The tea that saved Cartier and his men
was made from the eastern white-cedar.
It grows east from Manitoba and gets its
name from its pale wood. Deer eat its twigs
in winter.

Eastern white-cedars
are often used for
hedges.

Cedar wood is used for roof shingles,
poles and more. Long ago, people used
cedar poles to build the protective walls,
or stockades, around forts. Cedar strip
canoes are made from this tree's wood.
Birds and other animals depend on cedar
trees for food and shelter.

Canada's Provincial and

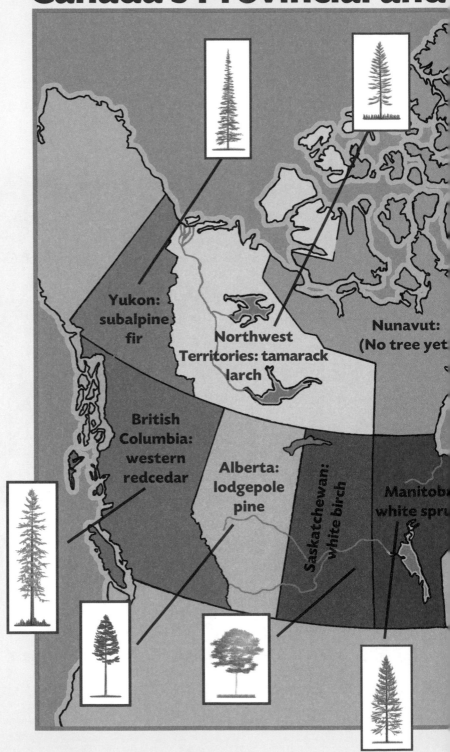

Yukon: subalpine fir

Northwest Territories: tamarack larch

Nunavut: (No tree yet

British Columbia: western redcedar

Alberta: lodgepole pine

Saskatchewan: white birch

Manitoba white spru

Territorial Trees

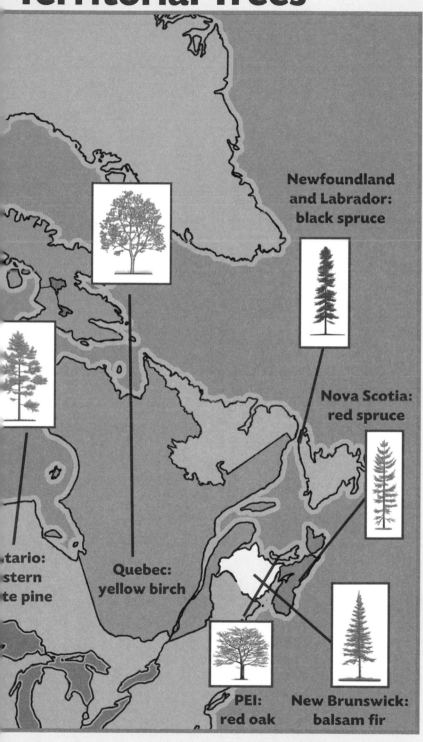

Newfoundland and Labrador: black spruce

Nova Scotia: red spruce

Ontario: eastern white pine

Quebec: yellow birch

PEI: red oak

New Brunswick: balsam fir

Glossary

Catkin: a cluster of tiny flowers, either in a short, fuzzy spike or slim, hanging bundle

Chlorophyll: the green colouring in leaves that plants use to make food

Coniferous: trees with cones and needle-shaped leaves. Most stay green all year. Cedars, firs, larches, pines and spruce are coniferous trees.

Cone: the part of a coniferous tree that contains the seeds

Crown: the top of a tree. Each tree species has a typical crown shape.

Deciduous: trees that lose their leaves in fall. Birches, maples, oaks, poplars and willows are deciduous trees.

Evergreen: trees that have green leaves throughout the year, including cedars, firs, pines and spruces

Forest: large area covered by trees

Fruit: the part of a deciduous tree that contains the seeds. It can be dry or juicy, brown or brightly coloured, prickly or smooth.

Lobe: part or section of a leaf. It can be rounded or pointed.

Native: trees that grow naturally in a place

Petiole: the small stalk attaching a leaf blade to a twig

Resin: a yellowish or brownish sticky liquid that oozes from most conifers and some deciduous trees

Samara: winged fruit. Also called a key.

Sap: fluid that transports water and nutrients through the plant

Species: a group of trees that have similar characteristics

Teeth: small pointed tips around the edge of a tree leaf

Tree: a plant with a woody trunk, grows to be at least 4.5 metres tall and can live for many years

Trunk: a tree's main stem that supports the branches and carries water, minerals and food between the roots and leaves

Index

Credits